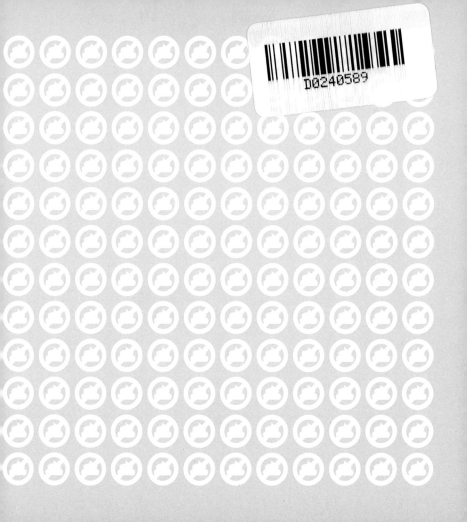

I SHIT YOU NOT

AN HACHETTE UK COMPANY
WWW.HACHETTE.CO.UK

SUMMERSDALE PUBLISHERS LTD
PART OF OCTOPUS PUBLISHING GROUP LIMITED
CARMELITE HOUSE
50 VICTORIA EMBANKMENT
LONDON
EC4Y 0DZ
UK

WWW.SUMMERSDALE.COM
PRINTED AND BOUND IN MALTA
ISBN: 978-1-78685-267-0

SUBSTANTIAL DISCOUNTS ON BULK QUANTITIES OF SUMMERSDALE BOOKS
ARE AVAILABLE TO CORPORATIONS, PROFESSIONAL ASSOCIATIONS AND
OTHER ORGANISATIONS. FOR DETAILS CONTACT GENERAL ENQUIRIES:
TELEPHONE: +44 (0) 1243 771107 OR EMAIL: ENQUIRIES@SUMMERSDALE.COM.

I SHiT YOU NOT

HUGH JASSBURN

HUGH JASSBURN HAS ROAMED THE EARTH RESEARCHING HIS BOOKS, AND ONE THING HIS EXTENSIVE TRAVELS HAVE TAUGHT HIM IS WHAT A WEIRD AND WONDERFUL WORLD WE LIVE IN. COUNTRIES BANNING LETTERS OF THE ALPHABET, THE ACCIDENTAL TEABAG, AND HAVE YOU EVER WONDERED HOW MANY HORSE POWER A HORSE HAS? READ ON, YOU'LL BE AMAZED – I SHIT YOU NOT…

1987 1988 1989
1990 1991 1992 1993
1994 1995 1996
1997 1998 1999 2000

**2013 WAS THE FIRST YEAR SINCE 1987
TO COMPRISE FOUR DIFFERENT NUMBERS**

2001 2002 2003
2004 2005 2006 2007
2008 2009 2010
2011 2012 2013

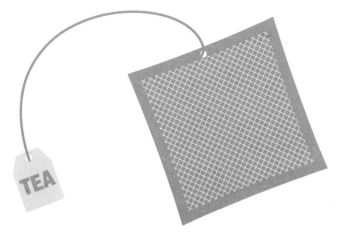

TEA

IN 1908 THOMAS SULLIVAN DISTRIBUTED
TEA LEAVES IN SMALL SILK BAGS
HIS CUSTOMERS DIDN'T REALISE THAT THE LEAVES
WERE SUPPOSED TO BE PUT IN METAL INFUSERS
AND PLACED THE BAGS DIRECTLY INTO HOT WATER.
SOON SULLIVAN WAS INUNDATED WITH ORDERS,
AND THE TEABAG WAS ACCIDENTALLY BORN.

I SHIT YOU NOT

Q

THE ONLY COUNTRY BEGINNING WITH A 'Q' IS QATAR

THE ONLY COUNTRY ENDING WITH ONE IS IRAQ

8

USE OF THE LETTER 'Q' WAS TECHNICALLY ILLEGAL IN TURKEY UNTIL 2013

IN 1928 LEADER MUSTAFA KEMAL ATATÜRK ALSO BANNED 'W' AND 'X' TO MOVE AWAY FROM THE ARABIC SYSTEM TO THE ROMAN ONE. IT WAS ARGUED THAT ROMANISATION WOULD HELP SPELLING, IMPROVE LITERACY AND REDUCE PRINTING COSTS.

SAINT-LOUIS-DU-HA! HA! IN QUEBEC,
CANADA IS THE ONLY TOWN IN THE WORLD WITH
TWO EXCLAMATION MARKS IN ITS NAME

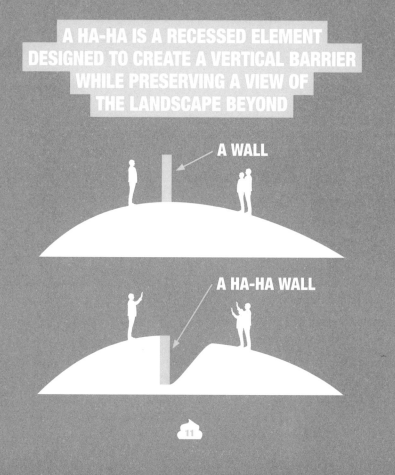

**COFFEE ISN'T MADE FROM COFFEE BEANS
THEY'RE SEEDS**

A STRAWBERRY IS NOT A BERRY
A BANANA IS

FINGERNAILS DON'T GROW AFTER DEATH
NEITHER DOES HAIR

YOUR TONGUE DOESN'T HAVE 'TASTE AREAS'
ALL PARTS DETECT ALL TASTES

15

YOU CAN'T SEE THE GREAT WALL OF CHINA FROM SPACE OR FROM THE MOON

EARTH IS CLOSER TO THE SUN IN JANUARY THAN JULY
THE RAYS' ANGLES, NOT DISTANCE, AFFECT TEMPERATURE

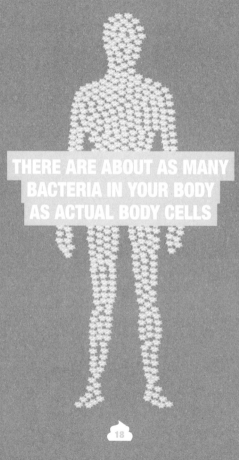

THERE ARE ABOUT AS MANY
BACTERIA IN YOUR BODY
AS ACTUAL BODY CELLS

THE SAUSAGE DOG OR DACHSHUND WAS FIRST BRED TO HUNT IN LOW, NARROW BADGER SETTS. 'DACHSHUND' TRANSLATES FROM GERMAN AS 'BADGER DOG'.

IN 2007 JEREMY HARPER FROM BIRMINGHAM, ALABAMA, COUNTED TO ONE MILLION LIVE ON A WEBCAM – IT TOOK HIM 89 DAYS

1–11,236	11,237–22,472	22,473–33,708	33,709–44,944	44,945–56,180
DAY 1	**DAY 2**	**DAY 3**	**DAY 4**	**DAY 5**
56,181–67,416	67,417–78,652	78,653–89,888	89,889–101,124	101,125–112,360
DAY 6	**DAY 7**	**DAY 8**	**DAY 9**	**DAY 10**
112,361–123,596	123,597–134,832	134,833–146,068	146,069–157,304	157,305–168,540
DAY 11	**DAY 12**	**DAY 13**	**DAY 14**	**DAY 15**
168,541–179,776	179,777–191,012	191,013–202,248	202,249–213,484	213,485–224,720
DAY 16	**DAY 17**	**DAY 18**	**DAY 19**	**DAY 20**
224,721–235,956	235,957–247,192	247,193–258,428	258,429–269,664	269,665–280,900
DAY 21	**DAY 22**	**DAY 23**	**DAY 24**	**DAY 25**
280,901–292,136	292,137–303,372	303,373–314,608	314,609–325,844	325,845–337,080
DAY 26	**DAY 27**	**DAY 28**	**DAY 29**	**DAY 30**
337,081–348,316	348,317–359,552	359,553–370,788	370,789–382,024	382,025–393,260
DAY 31	**DAY 32**	**DAY 33**	**DAY 34**	**DAY 35**
393,261–404,496	404,497–415,732	415,733–426,968	426,969–438,204	438,205–449,440
DAY 36	**DAY 37**	**DAY 38**	**DAY 39**	**DAY 40**
449,441–460,676	460,677–471,912	471,913–483,148	483,149–494,384	494,385–505,620
DAY 41	**DAY 42**	**DAY 43**	**DAY 44**	**DAY 45**

HE COUNTED FOR APPROXIMATELY 16 HOURS A DAY, AVERAGING JUST OVER 11,200 NUMBERS PER DAY

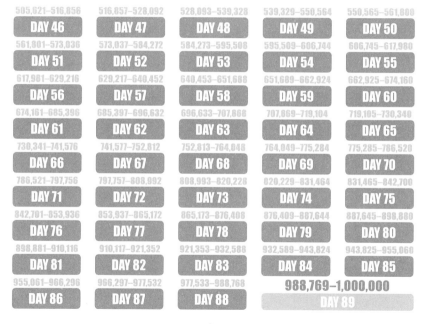

505,621–516,856	516,857–528,092	528,093–539,328	539,329–550,564	550,565–561,800
DAY 46	**DAY 47**	**DAY 48**	**DAY 49**	**DAY 50**
561,801–573,036	573,037–584,272	584,273–595,508	595,509–606,744	606,745–617,980
DAY 51	**DAY 52**	**DAY 53**	**DAY 54**	**DAY 55**
617,981–629,216	629,217–640,452	640,453–651,688	651,689–662,924	662,925–674,160
DAY 56	**DAY 57**	**DAY 58**	**DAY 59**	**DAY 60**
674,161–685,396	685,397–696,632	696,633–707,868	707,869–719,104	719,105–730,340
DAY 61	**DAY 62**	**DAY 63**	**DAY 64**	**DAY 65**
730,341–741,576	741,577–752,812	752,813–764,048	764,049–775,284	775,285–786,520
DAY 66	**DAY 67**	**DAY 68**	**DAY 69**	**DAY 70**
786,521–797,756	797,757–808,992	808,993–820,228	820,229–831,464	831,465–842,700
DAY 71	**DAY 72**	**DAY 73**	**DAY 74**	**DAY 75**
842,701–853,936	853,937–865,172	865,173–876,408	876,409–887,644	887,645–898,880
DAY 76	**DAY 77**	**DAY 78**	**DAY 79**	**DAY 80**
898,881–910,116	910,117–921,352	921,353–932,588	932,589–943,824	943,825–955,060
DAY 81	**DAY 82**	**DAY 83**	**DAY 84**	**DAY 85**
955,061–966,296	966,297–977,532	977,533–988,768	988,769–1,000,000	
DAY 86	**DAY 87**	**DAY 88**	**DAY 89**	

IN 1988 THE LARGEST EVER RECORDED TURTLE WAS WASHED UP ON HARLECH BEACH IN WALES. THE LEATHERBACK WAS ESTIMATED TO BE 100 YEARS OLD. IT WAS NEARLY 2.75 M IN LENGTH AND WEIGHED 914 KG.

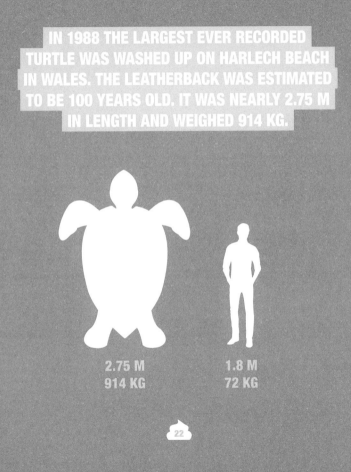

2.75 M
914 KG

1.8 M
72 KG

IRISH MILLIONAIRE MICHAEL O'LEARY ONCE OWNED A TAXI WITH A HACKNEY CARRIAGE LICENCE AND FITTED WITH A FARE METER SO THAT HE COULD USE THE BUS AND TAXI LANES IN DUBLIN

THE NORTH STAR
IS ESTIMATED TO BE
433 LIGHT YEARS
FROM EARTH

IF YOU COULD
STAND ON THE
NORTH STAR
WITH A
TELESCOPE
POWERFUL
ENOUGH
TO SEE
THE EARTH,
YOU WOULD
SEE IT AS IT WAS
IN THE LATE
16TH CENTURY

THE HUMAN BRAIN IS MUCH MORE ACTIVE AT NIGHT THAN DURING THE DAY

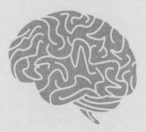

WHEN AWAKE, THE HUMAN BRAIN PRODUCES ENOUGH ELECTRICITY TO POWER A SMALL LIGHT BULB

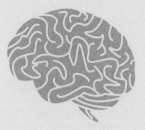

'SPHENOPALATINE GANGLIONEURALGIA' IS THE SCIENTIFIC TERM FOR BRAIN FREEZE

THE HUMAN BRAIN IS 10% SMALLER THAN IT WAS 20,000 YEARS AGO

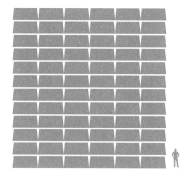

IT'S ESTIMATED THAT ALL OF THE GOLD EVER MINED WOULD FIT INTO A 20x20x20-METRE CUBE

HANDSHAKES WERE ORIGINALLY MEANT TO ENSURE SOMEONE WASN'T CARRYING A CONCEALED WEAPON

THE GRIP PROVED THAT THE HAND WAS EMPTY AND THE SHAKE WAS MEANT TO DISLODGE ANYTHING HIDDEN IN THE SLEEVE

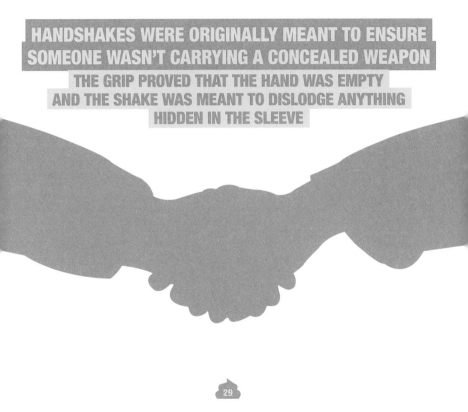

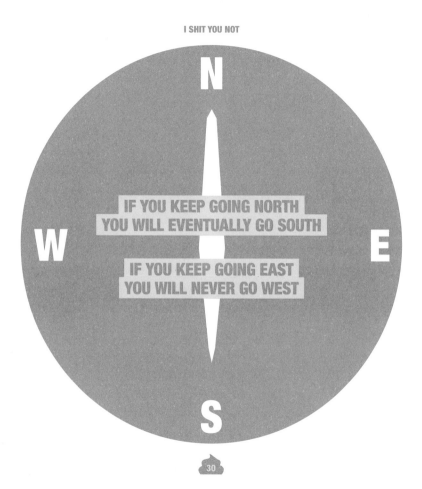

THERE'S A CATHEDRAL IN NEW ZEALAND MADE OF CARDBOARD TUBES

FOLLOWING THE 2011 EARTHQUAKE IN CHRISTCHURCH, NEW ZEALAND, 'DISASTER ARCHITECT' SHIGERU BAN WAS INVITED BY REV. CRAIG DIXON TO CREATE A CATHEDRAL FOR THE CITY. BAN COLLABORATED WITH CHRISTCHURCH FIRM WARREN AND MAHONEY AND BUILT THE STRUCTURE USING 86 CARDBOARD TUBES, WOOD AND GLASS.

A HOTEL IN SWEDEN MADE ENTIRELY OF ICE WAS CLOSED DUE TO IT NOT HAVING SMOKE DETECTORS

THERE ARE TWICE AS MANY KANGAROOS
IN AUSTRALIA AS PEOPLE

SUPERSTITIONS

AT MIDNIGHT ON NEW YEAR'S EVE IN SPAIN, EATING 12 GRAPES BRINGS 12 MONTHS OF GOOD LUCK

IT'S UNLUCKY TO WALK BACKWARDS IN PORTUGAL, AS IT SHOWS THE DEVIL YOUR PATH

IN EGYPT IT'S BAD LUCK TO OPEN A PAIR OF SCISSORS WITHOUT CUTTING ANYTHING – AND WORSE TO LEAVE THEM OPEN!

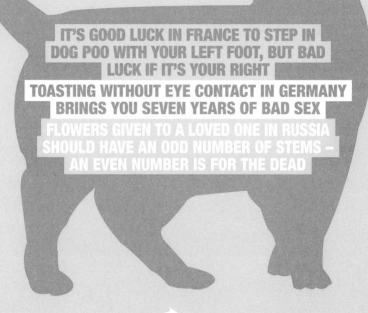

SUPERSTITIONS

IT'S GOOD LUCK IN FRANCE TO STEP IN DOG POO WITH YOUR LEFT FOOT, BUT BAD LUCK IF IT'S YOUR RIGHT

TOASTING WITHOUT EYE CONTACT IN GERMANY BRINGS YOU SEVEN YEARS OF BAD SEX

FLOWERS GIVEN TO A LOVED ONE IN RUSSIA SHOULD HAVE AN ODD NUMBER OF STEMS – AN EVEN NUMBER IS FOR THE DEAD

THE CRACK SOUND A WHIP MAKES
IS CAUSED BY A LOOP TRAVELLING ALONG
THE LENGTH UNTIL IT REACHES THE SPEED
OF SOUND AND CREATES A SONIC BOOM

1823
JOHANN WOLFGANG DÖBEREINER

1826
JOHN WALKER

AN OCTOPUS HAS THREE HEARTS

A GALLOPING HORSE PRODUCES 15–20 HORSE POWER

GOATS HAVE RECTANGULAR PUPILS

WHEN A MALE HONEY BEE CLIMAXES ITS TESTICLES EXPLODE AND IT DIES

PIG BEACH IS AN UNINHABITED ISLAND IN THE BAHAMAS – IT IS POPULATED BY A COLONY OF WILD PIGS THAT LIVE ON THE ISLAND AND IN THE SURROUNDING WATERS

THE SUN AND MOON APPEAR THE SAME SIZE BECAUSE THE SUN IS AROUND 400 TIMES FURTHER AWAY FROM EARTH THAN THE MOON, AND THE MOON IS ABOUT 400 TIMES SMALLER THAN THE SUN

LUNATIC

FROM THE LATIN 'LUNA' MEANING 'MOON' – IT WAS BELIEVED THAT INSANITY WAS CAUSED BY CHANGES IN THE MOON

JEANS

NAMED AFTER GENOA, ITALY – THEIR PLACE OF ORIGIN

MORTGAGE

FROM OLD FRENCH 'MORT GAIGE', MEANING 'DEAD PLEDGE', THE DEAL DIES IF THE DEBT IS PAID OR IF PAYMENT FAILS

DUNCE

AFTER SCOTTISH PHILOSOPHER JOHN DUNS SCOTUS, WHOSE THEORIES WERE DISCREDITED DURING THE 13TH CENTURY

GOODBYE

COMES FROM THE OLD ENGLISH PHRASE 'GOD BE WITH YE'

SALARY

FROM THE LATIN 'SALARIUM', WHEN ROMAN SOLDIERS WERE PAID AN ALLOWANCE TO BUY SALT

A CHICKEN LIVED FOR 18 MONTHS WITHOUT A HEAD

DURING SEPTEMBER 1945 LLOYD OLSEN AND HIS WIFE WERE KILLING CHICKENS ON THEIR FARM IN COLORADO, USA

ONE OF THE CHICKENS KEPT WALKING AROUND AFTER BEING DECAPITATED

AFTER A NIGHT IN A BOX ON THE PORCH THE CHICKEN WAS STILL ALIVE

OLSEN TOOK 'MIRACLE MIKE' AROUND THE AREA, BETTING WITH LOCALS THAT HE HAD A LIVE HEADLESS CHICKEN

MIKE THE HEADLESS CHICKEN FESTIVAL IS CELEBRATED EVERY YEAR IN COLORADO, USA

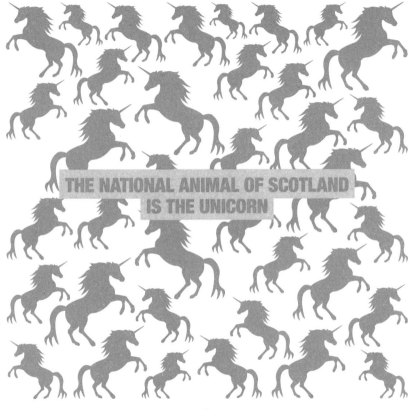

THE NATIONAL ANIMAL OF SCOTLAND
IS THE UNICORN

SNAKE CHARMING IS ILLEGAL IN INDIA

RUSSIA DIDN'T OFFICIALLY CLASSIFY BEER AS AN ALCOHOLIC DRINK UNTIL 2013

I SHIT YOU NOT

ONE MILLION BUBBLES WILL ESCAPE
FROM A GLASS OF CHAMPAGNE BEFORE IT'S FLAT

49

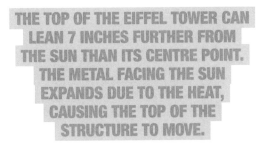

THE TOP OF THE EIFFEL TOWER CAN LEAN 7 INCHES FURTHER FROM THE SUN THAN ITS CENTRE POINT. THE METAL FACING THE SUN EXPANDS DUE TO THE HEAT, CAUSING THE TOP OF THE STRUCTURE TO MOVE.

IN 1923 JOCKEY FRANK HAYES WON
AT BELMONT PARK IN NEW YORK
EVEN THOUGH HE SUFFERED A HEART ATTACK
DURING THE RACE AND DIED – HIS BODY
STAYED IN THE SADDLE UNTIL HIS HORSE
'SWEET KISS' CROSSED THE FINISH LINE
FOR A 20–1 OUTSIDER VICTORY

THE LYRICIST OSCAR HAMMERSTEIN II IS THE ONLY PERSON CALLED OSCAR TO EVER WIN AN OSCAR

THE COLOSSAL SQUID HAS THE LARGEST EYES IN THE ANIMAL KINGDOM – THEY'RE THE SIZE OF BASKETBALLS

BABY TIGER SHARKS EAT EACH OTHER IN THE WOMB UNTIL ONLY ONE OR TWO SHARKS ARE BORN

SHEEP IN MAZES TEND TO TURN LEFT

A SCIENTIFIC STUDY SHOWED THAT WHEN GIVEN A CHOICE BETWEEN A LEFT OR RIGHT TURN, MOST SHEEP CHOSE LEFT

I SHIT YOU NOT

IN ONE YEAR LIGHT TRAVELS

5,878,499,817,000 MILES

DURING A LIFETIME, THE AVERAGE HUMAN WILL WALK A DISTANCE EQUIVALENT TO ABOUT FIVE TIMES AROUND THE EARTH

IN 1980 SADDAM HUSSEIN WAS GIVEN THE KEY TO THE CITY OF DETROIT

IN 1979 REV. JACOB YASSO OF DETROIT'S SACRED HEART CHALDEAN CATHOLIC CHURCH SENT A CONGRATULATORY MESSAGE TO THE NEW PRESIDENT OF IRAQ

SADDAM'S RESPONSE WAS A $250,000 DONATION TO THE CHURCH

IN 1980 YASSO TRAVELLED TO SADDAM'S PALACE IN BAGHDAD AS A GUEST OF THE IRAQI PRESIDENT

AT THE PALACE SADDAM ASKED YASSO ABOUT THE CHURCH'S DEBT AND HUSSEIN SOON DONATED ANOTHER $200,000

HUSSEIN REMAINS IN THE CITY'S EXCLUSIVE KEY-HOLDER CLUB ALONG WITH SANTA CLAUS, STEVIE WONDER AND ELMO

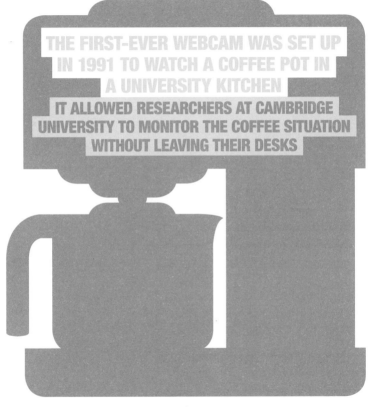

THE FIRST-EVER WEBCAM WAS SET UP
IN 1991 TO WATCH A COFFEE POT IN
A UNIVERSITY KITCHEN

IT ALLOWED RESEARCHERS AT CAMBRIDGE
UNIVERSITY TO MONITOR THE COFFEE SITUATION
WITHOUT LEAVING THEIR DESKS

IT'S ILLEGAL TO OWN JUST ONE
GUINEA PIG IN SWITZERLAND
GUINEA PIGS ARE SOCIAL ANIMALS
AND SUFFER FROM LONELINESS

ABCDEFGHIJKLMNOPQRSTUV
WXYZABCDEFGHIJKLMNOPQR
STUVWXYZABCDEFGHIJKLMN
OPQRSTUVWXYZABCDEFGHIJK
LMNOPQRSTUVWXYZABCDEFG
HIJKLMNOPQRSTUVWXYZABC

**ONE MILLION IS THE FIRST NUMBER THAT
CONTAINS THE LETTER 'M'**

DEFGHIJKLMNOPQRSTUVWXY
ZABCDEFGHIJKLMNOPQRSTU
VWXYZABCDEFGHIJKLMNOPQ
RSTUVWXYZABCDEFGHIJKLM
NOPQRSTUVWXYZABCDEFGHI
KLMNOPQRSTUVWXYZABCDEF

ABCDEFGHIJKLMNOPQRSTUV
WXYZABCDEFGHIJKLMNOPQR
STUVWXYZABCDEFGHIJKLMN
OPQRSTUVWXYZABCDEFGHIJK
LMNOPQRSTUVWXYZABCDEFG
HIJKLMNOPQRSTUVWXYZABC

THE ONLY NUMBER WITH LETTERS IN ALPHABETICAL ORDER IS 'FORTY'

DEFGHIJKLMNOPQRSTUVWXY
ZABCDEFGHIJKLMNOPQRSTU
VWXYZABCDEFGHIJKLMNOPQ
RSTUVWXYZABCDEFGHIJKLM
NOPQRSTUVWXYZABCDEFGHI
KLMNOPQRSTUVWXYZABCDEF

THE NOTE ASKED ANYONE WHO FOUND THE BALLOON TO WRITE TO HER

TEN DAYS LATER IT WAS FOUND 140 MILES AWAY IN PEWSEY, WILTSHIRE, BY ANOTHER LAURA BUXTON

BOTH LAURAS WERE TEN YEARS OLD, HAD A THREE-YEAR-OLD LABRADOR, A GUINEA PIG AND A RABBIT

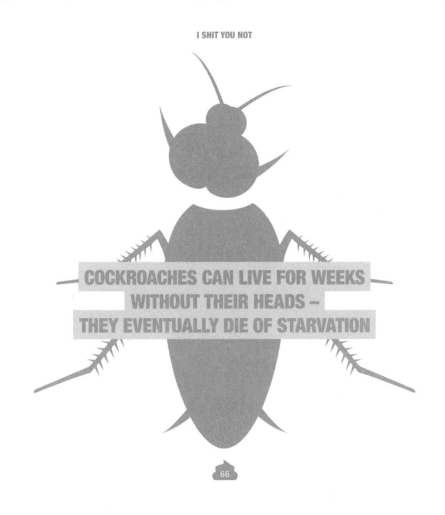

COCKROACHES CAN LIVE FOR WEEKS
WITHOUT THEIR HEADS –
THEY EVENTUALLY DIE OF STARVATION

BEFORE WW2 LOBSTER WAS CONSIDERED
THE COCKROACH OF THE OCEAN AND EATEN
BY THE POOR, HOMELESS, SLAVES AND PRISONERS

THE LONDON UNDERGROUND HAS THE BIGGEST LOST-PROPERTY OFFICE IN EUROPE

I SHIT YOU NOT

OVER 330,000 ITEMS ARE RECEIVED EVERY YEAR

13,000 KEYS

10,000 UMBRELLAS

46,000 BAGS

34,000 MOBILE PHONES

69

PIRATES WEARING EYE-PATCHES WEREN'T ONE-EYED

MOVING ABOVE AND BELOW DECKS FREQUENTLY MEANT GOING FROM BRIGHT LIGHT TO NEAR DARKNESS. KEEPING ONE EYE DARK-ADAPTED AND SWITCHING THE PATCH TO THE OTHER EYE WHEN GOING BELOW DECK ENSURED BETTER VISIBILITY.

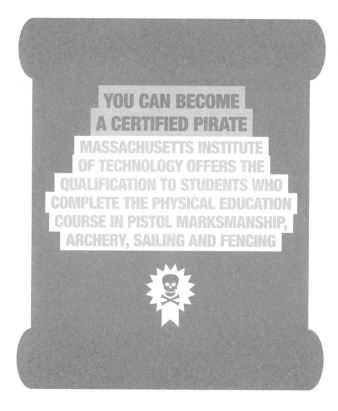

YOU CAN BECOME
A CERTIFIED PIRATE

MASSACHUSETTS INSTITUTE
OF TECHNOLOGY OFFERS THE
QUALIFICATION TO STUDENTS WHO
COMPLETE THE PHYSICAL EDUCATION
COURSE IN PISTOL MARKSMANSHIP,
ARCHERY, SAILING AND FENCING

BAKED BEANS

ARE NOT BAKED
THEY'RE STEAMED

72

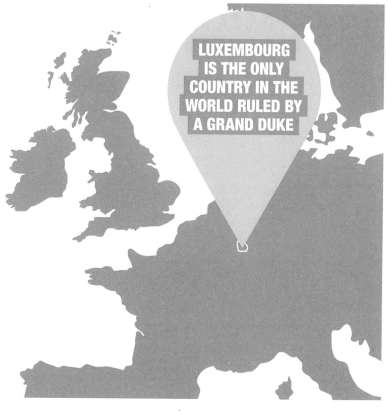

LUXEMBOURG IS THE ONLY COUNTRY IN THE WORLD RULED BY A GRAND DUKE

WAYNE ALLWINE MARRIED RUSSI TAYLOR IN 1991. WAYNE WAS THE VOICE OF DISNEY'S MICKEY MOUSE, RUSSI WAS THE VOICE OF MINNIE MOUSE.

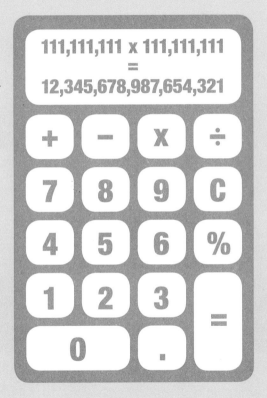

111,111,111 x 111,111,111
=
12,345,678,987,654,321

BETWEEN 1912 AND 1948
ART WAS A PART OF THE OLYMPICS

MEDALS WERE AWARDED FOR ARCHITECTURE,
LITERATURE, SCULPTURE, MUSIC AND PAINTING
FOR WORKS INSPIRED BY SPORTING THEMES

THE SUM OF ALL THE NUMBERS ON A ROULETTE WHEEL IS 666

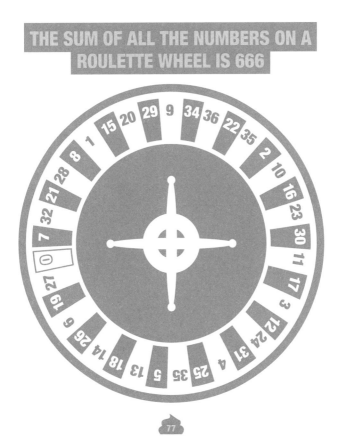

X2

IF YOU STARTED WITH A PENNY
AND DOUBLED YOUR MONEY EVERY DAY
YOU WOULD BE A MILLIONAIRE BY DAY 27

FLAMINGOS CAN ONLY EAT
WITH THEIR HEADS UPSIDE DOWN

IN 2007 HARRODS USED A COBRA TO PROTECT A £62,000 PAIR OF RUBY AND DIAMOND ENCRUSTED SANDALS

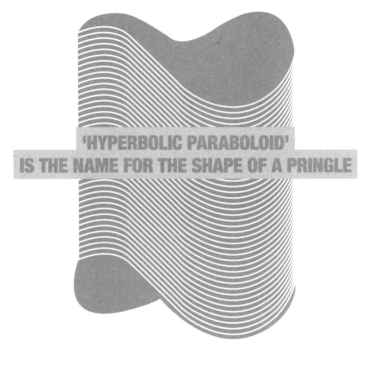

'HYPERBOLIC PARABOLOID' IS THE NAME FOR THE SHAPE OF A PRINGLE

'INTERGLUTEAL CLEFT'
IS THE MEDICAL NAME FOR ARSE CRACK

THERE ARE MORE STARS IN SPACE

I SHIT YOU NOT

THAN GRAINS OF SAND ON EARTH'S BEACHES

85

THE PHRASE 'WINNING HANDS DOWN' ORIGINALLY REFERRED TO A JOCKEY WHO WON A RACE WITHOUT WHIPPING HIS HORSE OR PULLING BACK THE REINS

A LITTLE VIAGRA DISSOLVED IN WATER KEEPS
FLOWERS UPRIGHT FOR LONGER

$TAR WAR$

IN 1977 20TH CENTURY FOX HAD SO LITTLE FAITH IN *STAR WARS* THEY GAVE AWAY CERTAIN RIGHTS TO GEORGE LUCAS INSTEAD OF INCREASING HIS DIRECTORIAL FEE. IN 2015 THE VALUE OF THE FRANCHISE WAS ESTIMATED AT $42 BILLION.

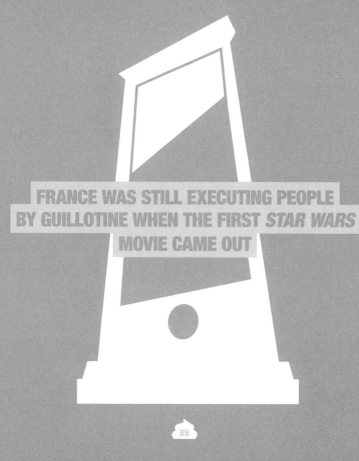

I SHIT YOU NOT

FRANCE WAS STILL EXECUTING PEOPLE BY GUILLOTINE WHEN THE FIRST *STAR WARS* MOVIE CAME OUT

89

NEPAL IS THE ONLY COUNTRY IN THE WORLD WITH A FLAG THAT ISN'T SQUARE OR RECTANGULAR

FOLLOWING NEWS THAT IT WAS THE SECOND-MOST CONFISCATED ITEM AT LONDON CITY AIRPORT, MARMITE PRODUCED 70 G HAND-LUGGAGE-FRIENDLY JARS

'YOU'RE TAKING THE PISS!'

DURING THE 1930s URINE WOULD BE TRANSPORTED ON CANALS TO WOOL MILLS IN NORTHERN ENGLAND TO BE USED AS DYE FIXERS

TRANSPORTING URINE WAS LESS LUCRATIVE AND RESPECTED THAN TRANSPORTING WINE

WHEN ASKED ABOUT THEIR CARGO, TRANSPORTERS WOULD OFTEN LIE AND SAY THEY WERE CARRYING WINE

IF THEY WERE NOT BELIEVED, THE RESPONSE WOULD BE 'NO, YOU'RE TAKING THE PISS'

ANOTHER WORD FOR URINE OR URINATION IS 'MICTURITION' WHICH LED TO THE TERM 'TAKING THE MIC' ALSO BEING USED

THE BUBONIC POPE

WHEN POPE GREGORY IX LINKED FELINES WITH DEVIL WORSHIP, CATS THROUGHOUT EUROPE WERE KILLED BY THE THOUSANDS. THIS LED TO A BOOM IN RAT NUMBERS AND THE SPREAD OF THE BUBONIC PLAGUE, KILLING AN ESTIMATED 200 MILLION PEOPLE.

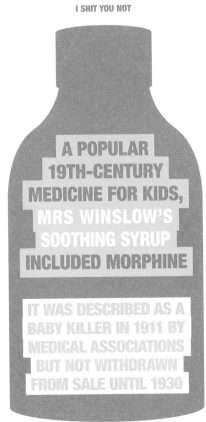

A POPULAR 19TH-CENTURY MEDICINE FOR KIDS, MRS WINSLOW'S SOOTHING SYRUP INCLUDED MORPHINE

IT WAS DESCRIBED AS A BABY KILLER IN 1911 BY MEDICAL ASSOCIATIONS BUT NOT WITHDRAWN FROM SALE UNTIL 1930

THERE ARE MORE THAN 45 MILLION DEAD PEOPLE ON FACEBOOK

AT SOME POINT IN THE FUTURE THERE WILL BE MORE DEAD USERS THAN LIVING ONES

BRIGHTWATER, NEW ZEALAND, HAD FIVE STREET LIGHTS IN 1911 AUTO-CONTROLLED BY CHICKENS

AT NIGHT, THE CHICKENS WOULD ENTER A COOP AND THEIR WEIGHT WOULD CLOSE AN ELECTRIC CIRCUIT, TURNING ON THE LIGHTS

IN 1956 McDONALD'S SUED A MAN LEGALLY NAMED RONALD McDONALD FOR CALLING HIS EATERY 'McDONALD'S FAMILY RESTAURANT'. THE REAL RONALD McDONALD WON.

A PREGNANT WOMAN IN BRITAIN CAN LEGALLY RELIEVE HERSELF ANYWHERE SHE WISHES

THE ORIGINAL MINI WAS DESIGNED WITH POCKETS IN ITS DOORS TO FIT A BOTTLE OF MILK OR GIN

AT A 1915 AUCTION, CECIL CHUBB BOUGHT STONEHENGE AS A GIFT FOR HIS WIFE – SHE WASN'T HAPPY, AS SHE'D SENT HIM TO BUY A SET OF DINING CHAIRS

DURING CHRISTMAS 2004 THE MILLENNIUM DOME WAS USED AS A SHELTER FOR THE HOMELESS

103

IN 2007
KEVIN SHELLEY
BROKE 46
WOODEN TOILET SEATS
WITH HIS HEAD IN
ONE MINUTE TO
CREATE A NEW
WORLD
RECORD

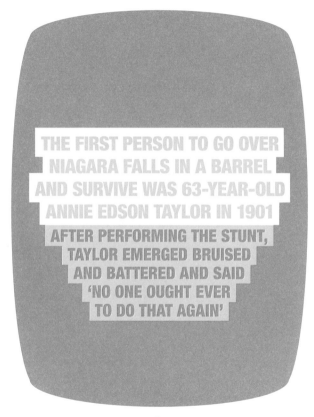

THE FIRST PERSON TO GO OVER NIAGARA FALLS IN A BARREL AND SURVIVE WAS 63-YEAR-OLD ANNIE EDSON TAYLOR IN 1901

AFTER PERFORMING THE STUNT, TAYLOR EMERGED BRUISED AND BATTERED AND SAID 'NO ONE OUGHT EVER TO DO THAT AGAIN'

I SHIT YOU NOT

A COMMON GARDEN SNAIL HAS MORE THAN 14,000 TEETH

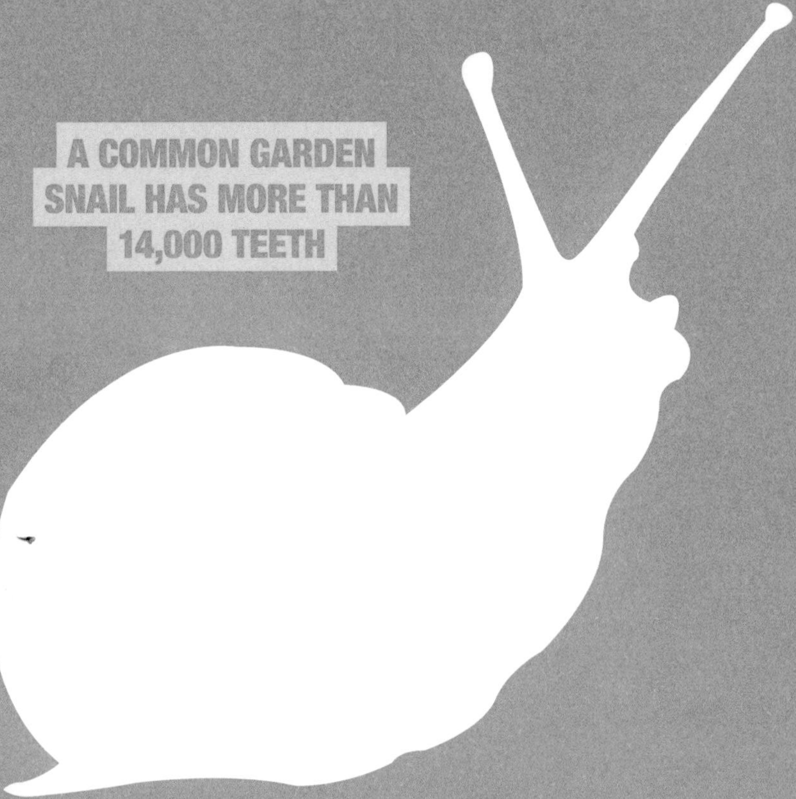

106

LEECHES
HAVE 32
BRAINS

IF YOU DIE IN AMSTERDAM
WITH NO FAMILY OR FRIENDS,
A POET WILL WRITE A POEM
AND READ IT AT YOUR FUNERAL

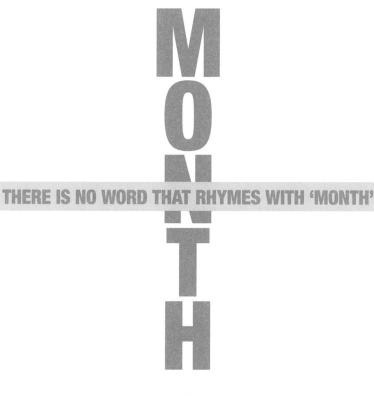

THERE IS NO WORD THAT RHYMES WITH 'MONTH'

THE CHANCELLOR OF THE EXCHEQUER
IS THE ONLY MEMBER OF THE
HOUSE OF COMMONS ALLOWED
ALCOHOL IN THE CHAMBER

IT'S ONLY ALLOWED DURING
THE DELIVERY OF THE BUDGET SPEECH

HMMMMMMMMMMMMMMMM
MMMMMMMMMMMMMMMM
MMMMMMMMMMMMMMMMM
MMMMMMMMMMMMMMMMM
MMMMMMMMMMMMMMMMM
MMMMMMMMMMMMMMMM

OH YEAH, ONE LAST THING...
YOU CAN'T HUM WHILE PINCHING YOUR NOSE CLOSED

MMMMMMMMMMMMMMMMM
MMMMMMMMMMMMMMMMM
MMMMMMMMMMMMMMMMM
MMMMMMMMMMMMMMMMM
MMMMMMMMMMMMMMMMM
MMMMMMMMMMMMMMMMM

IF YOU'RE INTERESTED IN FINDING OUT MORE
ABOUT OUR BOOKS, FIND US ON FACEBOOK
AT **SUMMERSDALE PUBLISHERS** AND FOLLOW
US ON TWITTER AT **@SUMMERSDALE**.

WWW.SUMMERSDALE.COM